Clip-Art Features for
Church Newsletters 4

Illustrations for Bulletin Boards,
Home Bulletins, and News Releases

Clip-Art Features for Church Newsletters 4

George W. Knight, Compiler
Howard Paris, Illustrator

BAKER BOOK HOUSE

Grand Rapids, Michigan 49516

Copyright © 1988 by Baker Books
a division of Baker Book House Company
P.O. Box 6287, Grand Rapids, MI 49516-6287

ISBN: 0-8010-5490-7

Fifth printing, February 1995

Printed in the United States of America

Contents

Introduction

As long as there are church newsletters, there will probably be an unquenchable need for brief, inspirational essays and fillers like those that appear in this book. We have already issued three previous books in this series: *Clip Art Features No. 1* (1984), *No. 2* (1986), and *No. 3* (1987)—and still churches are asking for more.

Like the other three books in this series, this compilation of new material contains scores of copyright-free items, complete with copy, illustrations, and borders. To give your newsletter a special touch, clip the features from the book and paste them down on your newsletter layout sheet. They are ready-made for reproduction by copying machine, electronic stencil, or offset press.

Thanks for your positive response to these practical newsletter aids. We are delighted they are being used so effectively to promote your church's work and to challenge church members to a deeper Christian commitment.

George W. Knight
Howard Paris

1

The Bible

The Bible Speaks

I am the Bible, God's wonderful library. I am always—and above all—the truth.

To the weary pilgrim, I am a strong staff.

To the one who sits in darkness, I am glorious light.

To those who stumble beneath heavy burdens, I am sweet rest.

To him who has lost his way, I am a safe guide.

To those who are sick in sin, I am healing strength and forgiveness.

To those who are tossed about by the storms of life, I am a steadfast anchor.

To those who search for salvation, I reveal the Savior of the world.

I am the Bible, God's wonderful gift to mankind.

Book of Strength

And should my soul be torn
  with grief,
Upon my shelf I find
A little volume, torn and
  thumbed,
For comfort just designed.

I take my little Bible down
And read its pages o'er,
And when I part from it I find
I'm stronger than before.
—Edgar A. Guest

My Daily Guide

Though the cover is worn
And the pages are torn,
   Though places bear traces of
    tears,
Yet more precious than gold
Is this Book worn and old
   That can shatter and scatter
    my fears.

This old Book is my guide;
It's a friend by my side;
   It will lighten and brighten my
    way;
And each promise I find
Soothes and gladdens my mind
   As I read it and heed it each
    day.
              —Author unknown

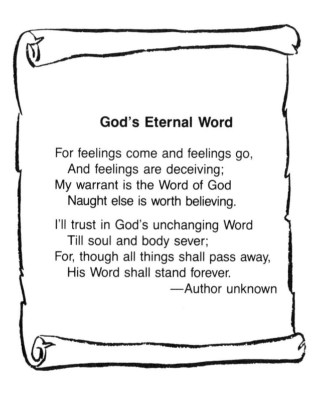

God's Eternal Word

For feelings come and feelings go,
  And feelings are deceiving;
My warrant is the Word of God
  Naught else is worth believing.

I'll trust in God's unchanging Word
  Till soul and body sever;
For, though all things shall pass away,
  His Word shall stand forever.
                    —Author unknown

2

Christian Ministry

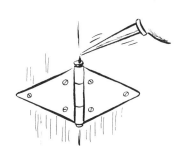

Oil-Can Christians

Perhaps you have heard the story about an eccentric man with a can of oil. He couldn't bear to hear a squeak or a rub, so he would stop to put a drop of oil on every squeaky hinge, door, gate, or latch that he passed.

This is a good illustration of what our lives as Christians should be like. Since we are ambassadors for Christ, one of our tasks is to serve as "lubrication for rusty hinges"—to take the love of Christ to those who are trapped in sin and caught in the webs of pessimism and despair.

This ministry is more than a responsibility; it's a genuine privilege that should make every Christian proud of his special calling as a disciple of Jesus Christ.

Things Undone

It isn't the thing you do;
   It's the thing you've left un-
      done
Which gives you a bit of heart-
      ache
   At the setting of the sun—
The tender word forgotten,
   The letter you did not write,
The flower you might have sent
   Are your haunting ghosts at
      night.
               —Margaret E. Sangster

"I'M LOOKING FOR SOMEONE IN NEED"

The Need Next Door

I said, "Yes, Lord, I'll go where you
    call me
    And I'll do what you want me to
    do."
But how could I know as I knelt
    there,
    That he'd ask me to stay here
    with you?

I thought surely he'd call me to
    China
    Or to Africa's far away shore.
I would gladly have sailed o'er the
    ocean,
    But he whispered, "I need you
    next door."

It's the faraway task that seems
    brightest
    And the grass seems more
    green o'er the way;
But how can he use me afar off,
    If I fail those I meet every day?

It's so easy to look past my neigh-
    bor
    Who has needs only God can
    supply;
God forgive me if I, like the Levite,
    Have been passing some
    suff'ring one by.
                    —Author unknown

The Gift of Encouragement

One of the most powerful things one person can share with another is *encouragement.* Encouragement can stop a suicide, a divorce, and countless other tragedies. A word of encouragement can heal someone who is broken and wounded. It can give someone the courage to keep trying.

Our world is full of negative, bitter, uncaring people who can't say anything good about anyone or anything. The people of God should be a radiant contrast to the people of the world. We should bubble over with the joy of the Holy Spirit. We should find it easy to be positive and uplifting. Are you an encouragement to those around you? Don't let someone die from neglect and lack of encouragement. Share your Christian joy!

3

Church Attendance and Support

Pulling Together in the Church

One draft horse working alone is a powerful animal that can pull a plow easily. But two draft horses properly harnessed and working together can triple and quadruple the amount of work that one alone can do.

This is a perfect picture of how a church should work. On our own we can accomplish a great deal for God's kingdom. But how much God multiplies our efforts when we work together toward a common goal and draw on the motivation and power of the Holy Spirit!

A Moneyless Operation Plan

Our finance committee has discovered a way for our church to operate without money. Here's how the plan will work:

Each member will use a broom and mop during the week to keep his part of the building clean. Then a paid janitor won't be necessary.

Each member will take his turn playing the organ and directing the choir. This means no organist or choir director will be needed.

Each member will spend at least a year as a missionary at his own expense on some foreign field. This will do away with the need for missions offerings.

If you don't like this plan for operating the church, give 10 percent of your income. Then we can conduct our ministry in the scriptural manner.

People Warmth

"People warmth" is that sense of comfort and joy that comes from being near loved ones and knowing that someone cares. Part of God's purpose in creating this church is to provide this kind of warmth for you. The Bible calls it *fellowship*—a supernatural closeness that exists between believers because God himself is in their midst. God has put us here so we can enjoy and benefit from this fellowship. And each church member supplies part of that warmth.

You are part of the fellowship of this church! Each time you attend, encourage someone, or join in the singing, you are building the warmth that makes our church special. Enjoy this warmth which God has provided. Warm your hearts with the love of God's people.

Productive Workers Needed

A farmer left his two sons, Ezekiel and Daniel, at home with instructions about the work to be done. When he returned, he found the work still not finished. Calling the two boys to account, he asked, "Ezekiel, what have you been doing today?"

"Nothin'" Ezekiel replied.

Then he asked Daniel, "And what have you been doing?"

"Helpin' Zeke."

Too many Christians today are "helpin' Zeke" when they should be totally involved and busy in the Lord's work. Our church has a place of service for every member. Get busy in some productive task that will bring honor and glory to the cause of Christ.

Mothball Christians

The United States has hundreds of ships which make up what is known as the "mothball navy." These ships are anchored in various harbors around the country. While they sit idle for the present moment, they can be prepared for combat on short notice. Military security demands that these ships be kept on standby, just in case they should ever be needed.

Many Christians these days also seem to be on "mothball" status. Most churches have dozens of members who never attend Bible study or worship services. They enjoy the privilege of church membership without contributing anything worthwhile to their church in return.

When Jesus calls us to become his disciples, he demands that we be on "active duty" at all times, ready to serve him with our time, talents, and material possessions. Let's put the "mothball mentality" behind us and sail out into the open waters of Christian service.

How to Find Your Way out of the "Woulds"

Some church members are hopelessly lost in the "woulds."

- I would go to Sunday school today, but I enjoy a little extra sleep on Sunday morning.
- I would take my children to Sunday school and church, but Sunday is my only day to play golf.
- I would teach a Sunday school class, but my job doesn't leave time for that.
- I would witness to others about Christ, but I don't know what to say.
- I would give more to the church, but there's nothing left after paying the bills.

The only way to find your way out of the "woulds" is to set your eyes on Christ and follow him. He will show the way.

THIS DO IN REMEMBRANCE OF ME

Approaching the Lord's Table

Come to this sacred table, not because you must, but because you may.

Come to testify not that you are righteous, but that you sincerely love our Lord Jesus Christ, and desire to be his true disciple.

Come, not because you are strong, but because you are weak; not because you have any claim on heaven's rewards, but because in your frailty and sin you stand in constant need of heaven's mercy and help.

Come, not to express an opinion, but to seek his presence and to pray for God's direction in your life.

The Lord's Day Is Special

There is something special about the early morning hours of a typical Sunday. Traffic is light, and the few people up at this hour seem to be in a friendly mood. All of God's creation seems to be at rest. The quiet, hushed reverence of a Sunday morning proclaims the truth that God is a living, active force in his world.

The best way to preserve the sanctity of Sunday is to seek God's presence in a house of worship. We will see you at church Sunday in a spirit of reverence and thanksgiving.

A Cure for Sunday Sickness

Morbus Sabbaticus is a disease peculiar to church members. The attack usually comes on suddenly every Sunday morning about 9:00 A.M. and lasts until around noon. In the afternoon patients are much improved. They are able to read the Sunday newspaper and participate in recreational activities.

The only known cure for *Morbus Sabbaticus* is for the church member to fix his or her eyes on Jesus Christ and to think seriously about the price he has paid for our redemption. The truly grateful Christian will be able to avoid this sickness and to wake up on Sunday morning looking forward to Bible study and worship in the Lord's house.

A "No-Excuse" Sunday

To increase attendance, churches should consider promoting a "no-excuse" Sunday. Here's how it would work:

Cots would be placed in the church hallways for those who say, "Sunday is my only day to sleep in." Hard hats would be provided for the people who say, "The roof would cave in if I ever came back to church." Blankets would be furnished for those who think the church is too cold; fans for those who say it's too hot. Hearing aids would be available for those who say the pastor speaks too softly and cotton balls for those who say he preaches too loudly.

Score cards would be furnished for those people who like to list all the hypocrites. A few unattached relatives would be in attendance for those who like to visit on Sundays. And one section of the church building would be landscaped with fake shrubbery and astroturf for the people who like to find God in nature on Sunday mornings.

Finally, the sanctuary would be decorated with Christmas poinsettias and Easter lilies for those people who have never seen the church without these special flower arrangements.

With all these typical excuses taken away, there should be a record attendance on "no-excuse Sunday."

God Builds No Churches

God builds no churches. By his plan
That labor has been left to man.
No spires miraculously arise;
No little mission from the skies
Falls in bleak and barren place
To be a source of strength and grace.
The humblest church demands its price
In human toil and sacrifice.

Men call the church the house of God
Toward which the toil-stained pilgrims trod
In search of strength and rest and hope,
As blindly through life's mists they grope.
And there God dwells, but it is man
Who builds that house and draws the plan;
Pays for mortar and the stone
That none need seek for God alone.

The humblest spire in mortal ken
Where God abides was built by men.
And if the church is still to grow,
Is still the light of hope to throw
Across the valley of despair,
Men still must build God's house of prayer.
God sends no churches from the skies—
Out of our hearts they must arise.
—Edgar A. Guest

Light for God's House

In a mountain village in Europe long ago, a nobleman wondered what gift he could present to his townspeople. At last he decided to build them a church.

No one saw the complete plans for the church until it was finished. When the people gathered, they marveled at its beauty. Then someone asked, "But where are the lamps? How will it be lighted?"

The nobleman pointed to some brackets in the walls. Then he gave each family a lamp, asking them to bring these with them each time they came to worship.

"Each time you are in church, the area where you are seated will be lighted," the noblemen said. "Each time you are not here, that area will be dark. This is to remind you that whenever you fail to come to church, some part of God's house will be dark."

How Large Should a Sunday School Class Be?

LARGE enough to provide a place of fellowship and support for each member, but small enough so the teacher will know and love each member.

LARGE enough that every new person will find a warm reception, but small enough so when even one member is absent, others will notice and care.

LARGE enough in its concern that members will reach out to the outsider, but small enough so there will be plenty of room for the new person who attends.

LARGE enough to allow many opportunities for participation and sharing, but small enough to provide a warm sense of fellowship among those present.

4

Family Life

To a Father
Who Was There

You were there when I was little
  To soothe my childhood fears;
There with love and wisdom
  To enrich my growing years.

When I came to you with prob-
  lems,
  You helped me work them out;
You were the one who taught me
  What life is all about.

You were there to show your
  pride
  On graduation day;
There to bless my marriage
  And give the bride away.

It seems that you have always
  played
  A most important part
In all the happy moments
  I hold within my heart.

Now I have a little one
  Who climbs upon your knee
And listens to the stories
  You used to tell to me.

And I'm happy you are here
  To soothe her childhood fears
And use your love and wisdom
  To bless her growing years.
                    —Alice E. Chase

To Know That You Are There

It isn't that we talk so much!
 Sometimes the evening through
You do not say a word to me;
 I do not talk to you.
I sit beside the reading lamp,
 You like your easy chair,
And it is joy enough for me
 To know that you are there!

It isn't that we go so much!
 Sometimes we like to roam
To concert or to theater,
 But best of all is home.
I sew a bit or read aloud
 A book we want to share,
And it is joy enough for me
 To know that you are there!

It isn't that you tell to me
 The thing I've come to know.
It goes too deep for words, I
 think,
 The fact you love me so.
You only have to touch my hand
 To learn how much I care,
And it is joy enough for me
 To know that you are there!
 —Anne Campbell

Definitions of a Dad

A dad is:
 A mender of toys, a leader of boys;
 A changer of fuses, a healer of bruises;
 A mover of couches, a healer of ouches;
 A hanger of screens, a counselor of teens;
 A pounder of nails, a teller of tales;
 A dryer of dishes, a fulfiller of wishes.
Bless him, O Lord, my Dad.
 —Jo Ann Heid

45

His Most Productive Crop

One growing season a farmer had a beautiful crop of grain. But a week before the harvest it was wiped out by a hailstorm. His son expected the farmer to lash out in bitterness and despair. But instead he accepted the loss in a spirit of faith and quiet acceptance.

Today this farmer's son is a person of faith who has also learned to live with failure and loss. He thinks of this devastated grain field as his father's most productive crop because it taught him a lesson he has never forgotten.

When it comes to our own children, we should remember that lessons and values which we try to teach them are more easily *caught* than *taught.* Modeling the right behavior before our children is a lot more effective than lectures and empty words.

The Joys of Motherhood

Dear Christian mothers, sing your
praise
Through all your busy, happy days
To God our Father, kind and good,
For all the joys of motherhood.

For that wee babe with smiling
charm
That softly nestles on your arm;
For childish laughter gay and
sweet,
And sounds of little scampering
feet.

For that young precious merry mite
Who walks with hand in yours held
tight;
And for the others older grown,
Who've learned to proudly walk
alone.

For blessings often mixed with
tears
As they mature through passing
years;
And that deep joy that naught can
dim,
When children give their hearts to
him.

Fear not the coming day to face,
For God will give you strength and
grace—
And hers shall be a great reward
Who trains her children for the
Lord.
　　　　　　—Margaret K. Fraser

A Father's Prayer

Give me, O God, the wisdom that I
need
To mold the tender lives within
my care;
Give me the power that I may sub-
tly lead
Them into righteousness—true
joy is there.

I ask for them no rainbowed path of
ease;
I ask for them no store of wealth
or fame;
I only ask that by their lives they
please
Thee and the world with an un-
tarnished name.

I know that man is weak, and life is
strong,
And sometimes honest roads
look very drear;
That winning laurels often takes
too long
And luring vistas from all sides
appear.

But while my young are still beneath my wing,
God, help me guide them right in
everything.
　　　　　　—Author unknown

49

5

Inspiration for Daily Living

Higher Thoughts

Lord, let me not be too
    content
with life in trifling service
    spent—
    Make me aspire!

When days with petty cares
    are filled,
Let me with fleeting thought
    be thrilled
    Of something higher!

Help me to long for mental
    grace
To struggle with the
    commonplace
    I daily find.

My little deeds not bring to
    fruit
A crop of little thought to suit
    A shriveled mind!
        —Author unknown

A Matter of Perspective

To make a large object appear smaller, just look at it
through the wrong end of a pair
of binoculars!

This is a good illustration of
how we as Christians should
deal with our problems. Deny-
ing that there is a problem
doesn't help. Christians have
difficulties just like everyone
else. But we do have a re-
source—faith in the Lord Jesus
Christ—that helps us deal with
our problems constructively so
that we aren't totally wiped out
by them.

The secret is to view our
problems in light of God's in-
finite grace and power. Our
problems are manageable
when we use these resources
that are part of the birthright of
every Christian.

Summertime Fun Overkill

Summertime is great because it offers us the opportunity to break the routine and get away for rest and relaxation. But some people work so hard at having fun during summer weekends that they have to drag themselves back to work on Monday morning!

These mad dashes to weekend fun spots only make us old and tired before our time. God's plan for a balanced life is for people to take time from their busy working lives to seek the peace and serenity of his presence in genuine worship.

Do take time for leisure and relaxation this summer. But remember that regular worship is also a part of God's re-creational plan for his people.

Silver Opportunities

During the California gold rush of the mid 1800s a group of miners laid claim to a promising area, only to realize later that it was useless because it had high concentrations of a peculiar black sand. They soon abandoned the claim to another wave of gold seekers.

The new settlers sent a sample of the black sand for scientific analysis. The test showed the substance was actually lead carbonate, loaded with silver. These miners eventually took a fortune in silver from the land that had been abandoned as useless just a few years before.

Sometimes we are just like those first miners—so busy looking for gold that we fail to recognize the rich silver deposits just beneath our feet. Opportunities for Christian service, rewarding involvement, and meaningful relationships lie all around us, if we will only take time to recognize their promise. Silver may not be as valuable as gold, but it will make you just as rich if you accumulate it in large amounts!

Life's Book

No matter what else you are doing
  From cradle days through to the end,
You are writing your life's secret story—
  Each day sees another page penned.

Each month ends a thirty-page chapter,
  Each year means the end of a part—
And never an act is misstated
  Or even one wish of the heart.

Each day when you wake, the book opens,
  Revealing a page clean and white—
What thoughts and what words and what
    doings
  Will cover its pages by night?

God leaves that to you—you're the writer—
  And never a word shall grow dim,
Till the day you write the word *Finish*
  And give your Life's Book back to him.
               —Author unknown

Hammer Christians

What we need are more Christians who quietly but effectively do their jobs like a hammer. A hammer keeps it head; it doesn't fly off the handle; it keeps pounding away; it finds the point quickly and drives it home; and perhaps most important, it is the only knocker in the world that accomplishes anything worthwhile!

Consider the hammer, and follow its example in your daily walk with Christ.

Gossiptown

Have you ever heard of Gossiptown
On the shore of Falsehood Bay,
Where Old Dame Rumor with rustling gown
Is going the livelong day?

It isn't far to Gossiptown
For people who want to go;
The idleness train will take you down
In just an hour or so.

The thoughtless road is crowded, you'll find,
For most folks start that way;
But it's all downhill and, if you don't mind,
You'll land in Falsehood Bay.

You glide through the valley of Wicked Talk,
And into the tunnel of Hate;
Then, crossing the Bitterness Bridge,
You walk through the city gate.

The principal street is called "They Say,"
And "I've Heard" is the public well,
And the breezes that blow from Falsehood Bay
Are laden with "Don't You Tell!"

In the midst of the town is Telltale Park—
You're never quite safe when there;
For its owner is Madame Suspicious Remark,
Who lives on the street "Don't Care."

—Author unknown

Message from the Bucket

Sometimes when you're feeling important,
Sometimes when your ego's in
bloom,
Sometimes when you take it for
granted
You're the best qualified in the
room.

Sometimes when you feel that your
going
Would leave an unfillable hole,
Just follow this simple instruction
And see how it humbles your
soul:

Take a bucket and fill it with water,
Put your hand in it up to the
wrist;
Pull it out and the hole that's re-
maining
Is the measure of how you'll be
missed.

You may splash all you please as
you enter—
You can stir up the water
galore—
But stop and you'll find in a minute
That it looks quite the same as
before.

The moral in this example
Is do just the best you can;
Be proud of yourself, but re-
member—
There is no indispensable man.
—Author unknown

The Last of the Ninth

The doctor knows what his trained eyes see,
And he says it is the last of the ninth for me;
One more swing while the clouds loom dark,
And then I must leave this noisy park.

'Twas a glorious game from the opening bell,
Good plays, bad plays, and thrills pell mell;
The speed of it burned my years away,
But I thank my God that he let me play!
—William F. Kirk

A Day Well Spent

If we sit down at set of sun
And count the things that we
    have done,
And counting, find
One self-denying act, one word
That eased the heart of one
    who heard;
One glance most kind
That fell like sunshine where it
    went—
Then we may count the day
    well spent.
           —Author unknown

Lesson from a Rose

It is only a tiny rosebud—
  A flower of God's design—
But I cannot unfold the petals
  With these clumsy hands of
  mine.

The secret of unfolding flowers
  Is not known to such as I—
The flower God opens so sweetly
  In my hands would fade and die.

If I cannot unfold a rosebud,
  This flower of God's design,
Then how can I think I have
  wisdom
  To unfold this life of mine?

So I'll trust him for his leading
  Each moment of every day,
And I'll look to him for guidance
  Each step of the pilgrim way.

For the pathway that lies before me
  My Heavenly Father knows—
I'll trust him to reveal the moments
  Just as he unfolds the rose.
           —Author unknown

Out in the Fields
with God

The little cares that fretted me
  I lost them yesterday
Among the fields above the sea,
  Among the winds at play.

Among the lowing of the herds,
  The rustling of the trees,
Among the singing of the birds,
  The humming of the bees.

The foolish fears of what might
    happen
  I cast them all away
Among the clover-scented grass,
  Among the new-mown hay.

Among the husking of the corn,
  Where drowsy posies nod,
Where ill thoughts die and good
    is born—
  Out in the fields with God.
      —Author unknown

Giving and Forgiving

What makes life worth the living
Is our giving and forgiving;
Giving tiny bits of kindness
That will leave a joy behind us.

For the little things are bigger
Than we often stop to figure;
What makes life worth the living
Is our giving and forgiving.
      —Thomas Grant Springer

Consolation

He knows, he loves, he cares;
Nothing this truth can dim.
He gives the very best to those
Who leave the choice with
him.
—Author unknown

View from the Hill

Worry is like a distant hill
We glimpse against the sky.
We wonder how we ever will
Get up a hill so high.

Yet, when we reach the top, we
see
The roadway left behind
Is not as steep and sheer as we
Have pictured in our mind.
—Author unknown

Careful Words

I'm careful of the words I say
To keep them soft and sweet;
I never know from day to day
Which ones I'll have to eat.
—Author unknown

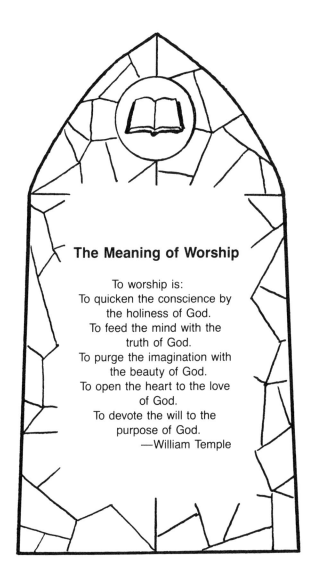

The Meaning of Worship

To worship is:
To quicken the conscience by
the holiness of God.
To feed the mind with the
truth of God.
To purge the imagination with
the beauty of God.
To open the heart to the love
of God.
To devote the will to the
purpose of God.
—William Temple

A Little More

We recall the kind old grocer
  When the sugar he would
    pour,
How he'd tip the scales to bal-
    ance,
  Then he'd add a little more.

And his business, how it pros-
    pered,
  Folks were always in his
    store,
For he gave an honest measure
  And he'd add a little more.

So it is with life, my brother,
  We will write a better score
When we've done what is ex-
    pected—
  If we'll add a little more.
                —Author unknown

Oceans of Ink

Could we with ink the oceans
    fill,
  And were the skies of parch-
    ment made,
Were every stalk on earth a
    quill,
  And every man a scribe by
    trade—
To write the love of God above
  Would drain the ocean dry;
Nor could the scroll contain the
    whole,
  Though stretched from sky to
    sky.
                —Author unknown

75

Transformation

A tiny egg once held a germ
That grew and grew into a
worm;
The worm grew bigger than its
skin,
And left the shell 'twas living
in;
And still it grew, until it spun
A chrysalis. Still life went on.

For from the chrysalis there
came
New life, but changed in form
and name.
With fluttering wings of beauty
rare
A butterfly rose in the air.

The worm it once was could
not guess
It ever would wear such a
dress,
For born within those tiny
germs
Is life beyond the dreams of
worms.
   —Jeanette Perkins Brown

Where Is God?

1. The LORD is **before** His people (Mic. 2:13; John 10:4).
2. The LORD is **behind** His people (Ps. 139:5).
3. The LORD is **above** His people (Deut. 33:12; Ps. 63:7; 91:1).
4. The LORD is **beneath** His people (Deut. 32:11; Isa. 40:11; 46:4).
5. The LORD is **around** His people (Ps. 125:2; 139:3).
6. The LORD is **with** His people (Num. 23:21; Matt. 1:23; 28:20).
7. The LORD is **in the midst of** His people (Isa. 12:6; Zeph. 3:17).

A Windshield View of Life

Everyone knows that the windshield in a car is much bigger than the rearview mirror. This is an excellent parable of the way we should approach life. Most of our attention should be focused on today's traffic—or the things that are happening right now—rather than on concerns from the past.

It's a good practice to glance in the rearview mirror now and then to see what's happening behind you. But we should never make the backward view our main concern. When we do, we become a danger to ourselves and others because we lose our awareness of the present moment and its significance.

Learn from the past, but live every day to its fullest as you claim the bountiful promises of God.

Not Growing Old

They say that I am growing old,
I've heard them tell it times untold,
In language plain and bold—
But I'm not growing old.
This frail old shell in which I dwell
Is growing old, I know full well—
But I am not the shell.

What if my hair is turning gray?
Gray hairs are honorable, they say.
What if my eyesight's growing dim?
I still can see to follow him
Who sacrificed his life for me
Upon the cross of Calvary.
—Author unknown

The Great "I AM"

As Christians, we need to remember that God is not known as the great *I WAS* but as the great *I AM* (see Exod. 3:14). The practical meaning of this truth is that we should not live in the past with its regrets and mistakes. Rather, we should emphasize the present with its opportunities and challenges. As the great *I AM*, God calls us to claim the promise of each new day and to live it fully for him.

The Power of the Bended Knee

Birds go to sleep on their perches, but they never fall off. This is because of the tendons in the bird's legs. They are so constructed that when the leg is bent at the knee, the claws contract and grip like a steel trap. The claws refuse to let go until the knees are unbent again. The bended knee gives the bird the ability to hold on to his perch so tightly.

Isn't this also the secret of the holding power of the Christian? Daniel found this to be true. Surrounded by a pagan environment, tempted to compromise with evil, urged to weaken his grip on God, he refused to let go. He held firm when others faltered because he was a man of prayer. He knew the power of the bended knee.

From sleeping birds we can learn the secret of holding things which are most precious to us—honesty, purity, thoughtfulness, honor, character. That secret is the knee bent in prayer, seeking to get a firmer grip on those values which make life worth living. When we hold firmly to God in prayer, we can rest assured he will hold tightly to us.

—Rollin S. Burhans

Sincere Prayer

'Tis not enough to bend the knee,
  And words of prayer to say;
The heart must with the lips agree;
  Or else we do not pray.

For words, without the heart,
  The Lord will never hear;
Nor will he to those lips attend,
  Whose prayers are not sincere.

—Author unknown

6

Interpersonal Relationships

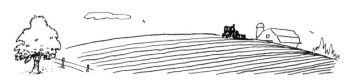

Going the Second Mile

A farmer left his son to plow a large field, instructing him to plow out to the peach trees and to try to finish the job by the end of the day.

When the farmer returned that evening, he discovered that his son had plowed all the way out to the road, far beyond the peach trees. It was almost twice the amount of work he had expected his son to do.

When he asked his son about it, the boy replied, "Dad, I plowed out to the peach trees because you told me to. But I plowed on out to the road because I wanted to."

The *wanted to* in this boy's response is the language of genuine love. Only the love of Christ within us can compel us to go beyond the requirements and give more than expected. Christians should pray daily for the love of Christ to direct us in all our dealings with others.

"And whoever compels you to go one mile," Jesus taught, "go with him two" (Matt. 5:41).

How to Find Friends

I went out to find a friend,
But could not find one there;
I went out to be a friend,
And friends were everywhere!
—Author unknown

Dealing with "Sandpaper" People

Sandpaper is a wonderful substance for working with wood. It removes all the rough spots, making wood as smooth as glass and just as nice to touch. But sandpaper is not nice if it is woven into the fabric of a person's personality.

"Sandpaper" people are those who rub us the wrong way. It could be anything from the way they wear their hair to the way they talk. Most of us can probably identify at least one person like this who taxes our patience and Christian spirit.

Perhaps it would help if we try to take a different view of these people. We should pray for such people and ask God to love them through us. This will help us to be more tolerant and forgiving in our attitude.

Giving Up the Grudge

A stranger looked on as a farmer struggled with a stubborn mule. "You could sure save yourself a lot of work by saying *Gee* and *Haw* to that mule instead of pulling on the lines," he advised.

"Reckon you're right," the farmer replied, "but this mule kicked me five years ago and I ain't spoke to him since."

In his attempt to get back at the mule, the farmer was actually creating a miserable situation for himself. That's exactly the way it is when we hold grudges against people for some wrong they have committed against us. By holding on to our hurt and looking for a chance to get even, we are actually giving them control over our behavior. Grudge-nursing, according to medical experts, can lead to health problems such as irrational behavior and stomach ulcers.

The Bible tells us a better way— give up the grudge, forgive the offender, and move on with our lives (*see* Mark 11:25; Col. 3:13).

7

Seasonal and Christian Year

The Gifts of the Animals

In a rude stable cold,
The friendly beasts their stories
  told:

"I," said the donkey, shaggy and
  brown,
"Carried his mother up hill and
  down,
Carried her safely to Bethlehem
  town."

"I," said the cow all white and red,
"Gave him my manger for his bed,
Gave him my hay to pillow his
  head."

"I," said the sheep, with the curly
  horn,
"Gave him wool for his blanket
  warm;
He wore my coat on Christmas
  Morn."

"I," said the camel, all yellow and
  black,
"Over the desert, upon my back,
Brought him a gift in the Wise
  Man's pack."

"I," said the dove, "from my rafter
  high,
Cooed him to sleep, that he should
  not cry,
We cooed him to sleep, my mate
  and I."

And every beast, by some good
  spell
In the stable darkness, was able to
  tell
Of the gift he gave to Emmanuel.
　　　　　　—Robert Davis

Annual
Christmas Journey

My feet are hearth-bound, to be
  sure,
But every Christmas Eve
I journey forth by land, by sea
(Nor height nor depth can hinder
  me).

Until a hallowed spot I gain:
A sheepcote on a plain.
I sit with shepherds by the fire,
I hear the tales they weave.

And when the huddled sheep are
  still,
Amazed, I watch God's glory fill
The night; there kneel while seraphs
  tell
Of Christ Emmanuel.

I cherish every accent pure,
With shepherds, too, believe;
I follow to the lowly bed
And find him as the angel said.

In swaddling clothes, in light divine,
His manger is my shrine;
Feet hearth-bound, but oh, what
  flight
A soul may take by Christmas
  light!
　　　　　　—Dorothy Lehman Sumerau

Telling the Christmas Story

Have you shared the Christmas
   story?
   Have you told its message true?
There are others who would gladly
   Hear the word of life from you.

Have you told them how the angels
   To the humble shepherds came?
Have you given them the tidings
   That the herald did proclaim?

Have you told them how the radi-
   ance
   From the Christmas star did
   guide
The band of seeking Magi
   To the little Christ-Child's side?

Have you told them how this Jesus
   Was the Savior long-foretold
And to him they brought rich tribute
   Of myrrh, frankincense, and
   gold?

Have you told them he's the Savior
   Who alone redeems from sin?
Have you told them he can give
   them
   Peace and joy and love within?

If you have, then you will surely
   Know the bliss of love sublime;
And if not, oh, haste to share it
   While the bells of Christmas
   chime.
           —Author unknown

The Many Meanings of Christmas

CHRISTMAS is the glow that warms the hearts of people wherever the message of "peace on earth to men of goodwill" is believed.

CHRISTMAS is peace in a world where people have been alienated from each other by hatred and jealousy.

CHRISTMAS is love that flows from one heart to another.

CHRISTMAS is giving, sharing, lifting, caring, and being what Christ wants us to be.

CHRISTMAS is giving to those who cannot give to us. It is visiting the neglected, lifting the fallen, giving hope to the hopeless, assuring victory to the defeated.

CHRISTMAS is surrender of one's life to Christ in renewed dedication, making Christ the Lord of our lives.

A Child of Hope

To us a child of hope is born,
  To us a son is given;
Him shall the tribes of earth obey,
  Him, all the host of heaven.

His name shall be the Prince of
    Peace,
  Forevermore adored;
The Wonderful, the Counselor,
  The great and mighty Lord.

His power, increasing, still shall
    spread;
  His reign no end shall know;
Justice shall guard his throne
    above,
  And peace abound below.

To us a child of hope is born,
  To us a son is given;
The Wonderful, the Counselor,
  The mighty Lord of heaven.
          —Author unknown

I Am the Flag

I am the flag of the United States of America. I was born on June 14, 1777, in Philadelphia. There the Continental Congress adopted my stars and stripes as the national flag.

My thirteen stripes alternating red and white, with a union of thirteen white stars in a field of blue, represented a new constellation, a new nation dedicated to the personal and religious liberty of mankind. Today fifty stars signal from my union—one for each of the fifty sovereign states in the greatest constitutional republic the world has ever known.

My colors symbolize the patriotic ideals and spiritual qualities of the citizens of my country.

My red stripes proclaim the fearless courage and integrity of American men and boys and the self-sacrifice and devotion of American mothers and daughters.

My white stripes stand for liberty and equality for all.

My blue is the blue of heaven, loyalty, and faith.

I am the flag. I symbolize all that is uplifting and good about our country.

The Legend of Uncle Sam

Just how did the familiar cartoon character, Uncle Sam, come to be identified as a symbol of the United States?

No one knows for sure. But one theory is that Uncle Sam evolved from an actual person, businessman Samuel Wilson of Troy, New York, who was nicknamed "Uncle Sam." Wilson supplied barrels of beef to the United States army during the War of 1812. He stamped these barrels with "U.S." to indicate they were government property, but the soldiers on the front line dubbed the barrels as food from "Uncle Sam." The nickname eventually came to be attached to the United States itself.

The cartoon figure of Uncle Sam as a goateed gentleman with top hat, bow tie, and striped pants evolved across several decades as political cartoonists depicted the United States through this drawing. But the one cartoonist credited with crystalizing this figure and giving it the touches that are still used today was Thomas Nast, a popular cartoonist of the late 1800s.

This cartoon symbol has been around a while, and so has the nation he represents. Long live Uncle Sam and the Christian ideals on which our great nation is founded!

Resurrection Living

For resurrection living
 There is resurrection power,
And the praise and prayer of trusting
 May glorify each hour.

For common days are holy
 And years an Eastertide
To those who with the living Lord
 In living faith abide.
 —Author unknown

One Solitary Life

He was born in an obscure village, the child of a peasant woman. He grew up in still another village, where he worked in a carpenter shop until he was thirty. Then for three years he was an itinerant preacher. He never wrote a book; he never held an office. He never had a family or owned a house. He didn't go to college. He never visited a big city.

He never traveled more than two hundred miles from the place where he was born. He did none of the things one usually associates with greatness. He had no credentials but himself. He was only thirty-three when the tide of public opinion turned against him. His friends ran away.

He was turned over to his enemies and went through the mockery of a trial. He was nailed to a cross between two thieves. While he was dying, his executioners gambled for his clothing—the only property he had on earth. After he died, he was laid in a borrowed grave through the pity of a friend.

Nineteen centuries have come and gone, and today he is the central figure of the human race and the leader of mankind's progress. All the armies that ever marched, all the navies that ever sailed, all the parliaments that ever sat, all the kings that ever reigned, put together, have not affected the life of man on this earth as much as that one solitary life.

—Henry Drummond

He Lives Within

How do I know that Christ is
    risen?
What proof have I to give?
He touched my life one blessed
    day
And I began to live.

How do I know he left the tomb
That morning long ago?
I met him just this morning
And my heart is still aglow.

How do I know that endless life
He gained for me that day?
His life within is proof enough
Of immortality.

How do I know that Christ still
    lives
Rich blessings to impart?
He walks with me along the way
And lives within my heart.
            —Author unknown

Guidance Through the Year

In faith, O Lord, you guided
me
  Through every day of the
  year;
Come blinding storm, come
doubt or pain,
  Your hand was always near.

The year was long, each day
unknown,
  Till I had trod it through;
But ever did I walk secure
  Because you walked there,
  too.

That year is past and all its
days,
  Now finished, lie behind;
But reaching out ahead of me
  A strange new year I find.

So strange, untried, these
newer days—
  But, Lord, I have no fear—
For I know well that every
hour
  Your presence will be near.
                    —Lois Snelling

Tomorrow's Way

I know not if tomorrow's way
  Be steep or rough;
But when his hand is guiding
  me,
  That is enough.

And so, although the veil has
  hid
  Tomorrow's way,
I walk with perfect faith and
  trust
  Through each today.

The love of God has hung a
  veil
  Around tomorrow
That we may not its beauty
  see
  Nor trouble borrow.

But oh! tis sweeter far to trust
  His unseen hand,
And know that all the paths of
  life
  His wisdom planned.
                    —Author unknown

Thanksgiving Gifts

I thank thee for these gifts, dear
God,
Upon Thanksgiving Day—
For love and laughter and the
faith
That makes me kneel to pray.

For life that lends me hap-
piness,
And sleep that gives me
rest—
These are the gifts that keep
my heart
Serene within my breast.

Love, laughter, faith, and life
and sleep,
We own them, every one—
They carry us along the road
That leads from sun to sun.
—Margaret E. Sangster

A Thanksgiving Psalm

O come, let us sing unto the
Lord; let us make a joyful noise
to the rock of our salvation. Let
us come before his presence
with thanksgiving, and make a
joyful noise unto him with
psalms.

For the Lord is a great God,
and a great King above all
gods. In his hand are the deep
places of the earth: the strength
of the hills is his also. The sea
is his, and he made it: and his
hands formed the dry land.

O come, let us worship and
bow down: let us kneel before
the Lord our maker. For he is
our God; and we are the people
of his pasture, and the sheep of
his hand.

Psalm 95:1-7

8

Witnessing and Evangelism

Four Witnessing Essentials

Successful witnessing depends on four essential ingredients:

1 The joy you have in your own heart. If you are thrilled to be a Christian, you won't have trouble convincing lost people of the value of accepting Christ.

2 The purity of your own life. If your own life is right with God, lost people will listen to what you have to say. If your life is stained with sin, your testimony for Christ will be weakened.

3 Your ability to use the Bible. The successful Christian witness has to know his Bible. With a thorough knowledge of God's Word, you should be able to answer the questions and excuses put forward by the unsaved.

4 Your willingness to try. You can't win others to Christ if you don't make the effort! Catch the vision. Talk about Jesus to everyone you meet. Winning others to Christ is one of the greatest joys in life.

The Master Key

Most large buildings have keys for every door in the building. But there is usually one key which fits every door. It's called the master key.

In a church there are many keys to various activities and ministries. But there is one key which fits everything. It's called visitation.

Visitation is the key to Sunday school growth. It's the key to revival, evangelistic outreach, and successful soul-winning. Visitation is the keynote in our Lord's commission, "Go ye into all the world and preach the gospel."

Definitions of Witnessing

WITNESSING is the militant sound of tramping feet, searching for lost people in the alleyways of life.

WITNESSING is a tender touch, a hand extended to a person on the edge of indecision and despair.

WITNESSING is a warm appeal to empty lives to come to the richness of new life in Jesus Christ.

WITNESSING is meeting people with a handshake, a bit of conversation, and a friendly invitation to visit your church.

WITNESSING is telling others about Jesus Christ and his power to redeem.

Who Are My Neighbors?

N is for neighbor. Many of us have neighbors who are not actively involved in church or Sunday School.

E is for employees and employers. Are all the people you work with actively involved in a church?

I is for interesting people. Every day we meet a lot of interesting people who are not actively involved in church or Bible study.

G is for general contacts—people at the bank, spa, classroom, service station, or grocery store.

H is for hobby friends—people who share our interest in antiques, needlecraft, stamp collecting, etc.

B is for baby. New babies are born daily, and this is a natural time for parents who have been inactive to get involved in church again.

O is for occupational friends—people in the workplace who admire and respect you.

R is for relatives—children, parents, brothers, in-laws, etc.

This list shows that you as a Christian really do have a wide circle of influence. Share your witness with these neighbors. Let them know that God cares for them.